"**This book offers great insights** into what's necessary to effectively value and manage creativity in the workplace. It helps people understand the dynamics of innovation and challenges us to embrace the opportunities that all our employees bring us."

— HAROLD W. BURLINGAME
Executive Vice President, AT&T

"**Congratulations on giving us a new motto:**
'*E Pluribus Maximus* (Greatness from Many)'!
This is a commandment for today's organizations."

— BARRY Z. POSNER
Coauthor of *The Leadership Challenge* and *Credibility*

"**A Peacock in the Land of Penguins is a wonderful fable** for individuals and organizations striving to flourish in a fast-changing world. While it may ruffle some feathers, a valuable message is delivered with wit and humor."

— PHYLLIS PFEIFFER
Vice President, Advertising and Marketing,
Contra Costa Times, California

D0067021

"A Peacock in the Land of Penguins is a beautiful **metaphor** that goes to the heart of today's issues and concerns. The added quiz, checklists, how-tos, practical tips, and suggestions in the revised edition are important aids to anyone interested in working with and understanding people from a fresh perspective. It's a must-read!"

— PHILLIP R. WALKER, Ph.D.
President, Walker International, Inc.,
consultant to NASA Lewis Research Center

"I loved it! This is an engaging tale of the challenges and dilemmas faced by those who are 'different' as they struggle for success and fulfillment — as well as the challenges and dilemmas of those who are members of the power elite in today's organizations. Truly a fable for our times!"

— JUDY B. ROSENER
Professor of Business at the University of California, Irvine,
author of *America's Competitive Secret: Utilizing Women
as a Strategic Management Tool*

"Is there anyone among us who has not, at one time or another, felt the pain and frustration of not being appreciated for who they really are? *A Peacock in the Land of Penguins,* a powerful message, simply told, speaks to the spirit in each of us that yearns to fly high and free."

— LAURIE BETH JONES
Author of *Jesus, CEO* and *The Path*

"I have been part of penguin organizations and watched disasters result from management's lack of openness to new ideas. They would have saved tens of millions by paying attention to this simple little book."

— JAMES B. SHAFFER
CEO, Clickshare Service Corporation,
former CEO, Guy Gannett Communications

"What a wonderful book! It offers a cautionary tale for managers and executives everywhere about the meaning and importance of new perspectives for successful businesses today. It should be required reading!"

— BOB NELSON
Author of *1001 Ways to Reward Employees*
and *Managing for Dummies*

"*A Peacock in the Land of Penguins* made me laugh and cry. I laughed as you so simply revealed the 'bottom line' about my experience at my previous company. I cried for all the valuable years I lost trying to become a penguin."

— LINDA SINILA
Former California mortgage broker

Third edition

A peacock IN THE
LAND OF PENGUINS

A Fable about Creativity & Courage

BJ Gallagher Hateley
and Warren H. Schmidt

Illustrations by Sam Weiss
Foreword by Ken Blanchard

BK

BERRETT-KOEHLER PUBLISHERS, INC.
San Francisco

Berrett-Koehler Publishers, Inc.
235 Montgomery Street, Suite 650
San Francisco, CA 94104-2916
Tel: (415) 288-0260
Fax: (415) 362-2512
www.bkconnection.com

ORDERING INFORMATION

Quantity sales. Special discounts are available on quantity purchases by corporations, associations, and others. For details, contact the "Special Sales Department" at the Berrett-Koehler address above.

Individual sales. Berrett-Koehler publications are available through most bookstores. They can also be ordered direct from Berrett-Koehler: Tel: (800) 929-2929; Fax: (802) 864-7626; www.bkconnection.com

Orders for college textbook/course adoption use. Please contact Berrett-Koehler: Tel: (800) 929-2929; Fax: (802) 864-7626.

Orders by U.S. trade bookstores and wholesalers. Please contact Publishers Group West, 1700 Fourth Street, Berkeley, CA 94710. Tel: (510) 528-1444; Fax (510) 528-3444.

Printed in the United States of America

Printed on acid-free and recycled paper that is composed of 80% recovered fiber, including 30% post consumer waste.

Library of Congress Cataloging-in-Publication Data
Hateley, B. J. Gallagher (Barbara J. Gallagher), 1949-
A peacock in the land of penguins: a fable about creativity and courage / BJ Gallagher Hateley, Warren H. Schmidt; illustrated by Sam Weiss. — 3rd ed.
    p. cm.
Includes bibliographical references.
ISBN 1-57675-173-2
    1. Pluralism (Social sciences) — Fiction. 2. Diversity in the workplace — Fiction. 3. Management — Fiction. I. Schmidt, Warren H. II. Title.
PS3358.A7378 P43 2001
813'.54–dc21   2001043241

Third Edition

  06   05   04   03   10   9   8   7   6   5   4

Cover and book design: Mary Sanichas, Oakland, CA
Copy editing: Elissa Rabellino, San Rafael, CA

We dedicate this book

to all who yearn to fly free

and show their true colors —

and to all who have the wisdom to learn

from those who are different

Contents

Part I: A Peacock in the Land of Penguins

Part II: Tips and Tools for Feathered Friends

**Part III: Ideas and Examples
  for Teaching Penguins to Fly**

**Part IV: Additional Resources for Peacocks
  and for Penguins**

A Note from the Authors
About This Expanded Edition

When we first began writing this parable about a peacock in the Land of Penguins several years ago, little did we know where the book would ultimately take us! We knew we had an important message about creativity and innovation in the context of today's organizations — and we wanted to express it in a way that would entertain as well as enlighten. We wanted to write a story that would speak to both the hearts and minds of people.

However, we had no idea how popular the book would become, and that it would evolve into a veritable cottage industry. We now have translations into many languages worldwide, a best-selling video that is used in conferences and seminars, assessment instruments for consultants and trainers, and a whole world of merchandising — T-shirts, coffee mugs, feather pens, penguin stress toys, and more!

Since its first publication in January 1995, many of our readers have asked us for more information; they want ideas and suggestions about what to do with the insights from our book. "How can I deal with my own situation?" they ask. Managers and executives also ask: "Can you help me transform my organization?"

This expanded version is our answer to their questions. We have revised and expanded Part II: "Tips and Tools for Feathered Friends" — advice to peacocks struggling to find happiness and success at work. And we have added a *new* section, Part III: "Ideas and Examples for Teaching Penguins to Fly" — advice to penguins who want to transform their organizations by embracing new ideas (sometimes from unlikely sources). We've also expanded our Part IV: "Resources" section, including training materials, videos, and merchandise to help reinforce the message of the *Peacock* story. We hope you will find these new additions helpful!

> BJ Gallagher Hateley
> Warren H. Schmidt
> Los Angeles, California
> September 2001

Foreword

Every once in a while a small book comes along that deals with a profound subject in a simple, elegant way. *A Peacock in the Land of Penguins* is such a book. I loved this book when the first edition came out in 1995, and I love this new edition even more. It provides important insights into the issue of creativity and innovation in the workplace — and it does so in a most engaging manner. Through the medium of a fable, this book helps us to see what can happen when we try to express ourselves fully and courageously in an environment created by executives and managers who view the world very differently.

Stories are a great way to convey important messages — they inspire and teach at the same time. People forget facts, figures, and theories, but they remember stories. People who know me can tell you how often I use stories in my own conversations, in my speeches, and in my daily life. I love to write great stories, and I love to read great stories.

This is the story of Perry the Peacock — a bright, talented, colorful bird — who comes to live in the Land of Penguins. He soon runs into problems because the penguins have established a chilly organizational climate that is formal, bureaucratic, and governed by a vast array of written and unwritten rules. Although his talent is recognized, his different and unusual style makes the penguins feel uneasy. The very thing he was recruited for — his distinctive flair and creativity — is now viewed as a problem by the penguins, once Perry is inside the organization!

His experience reflects that of "birds of different feathers" in many of today's organizations. Executives and managers *say* that they want new ideas and new thinking from their employees, but their actions indicate otherwise. New ideas are disruptive, they're messy, they challenge the status quo, they require taking chances and increased risk, and they push everyone out of their comfort zones. So people who are different, people with new views on how to make the organization successful, are often discouraged from expressing them — much to the detriment of both the individual and the organization.

This delightful corporate fable follows the adventures of Perry the Peacock and other exotic birds as they try to make their way in the Land of Penguins. Their story is both entertaining and enlightening. This is a tale of the perils and possibilities of being unique and creative in a world that values comfort, safety, and the predictability of conformity.

If you're interested in new ideas for making yourself and your organization successful, read this little book. Creating a workplace where creativity and innovation can flourish is a top priority for managers and employees alike. There are important insights for all of us!

Ken Blanchard
coauthor of *The One Minute Manager*

Part I
The Story

There once was a time,
in the not so distant past,
when penguins ruled many lands
in the Sea of Organizations.

These penguins were not always wise,
they were not always popular,
but they were always in charge.

Most organizations looked the same:

Top executives
and managers
wore their distinctive penguin suits,
while worker birds
of many kinds
wore colors and outfits
that reflected their work
and their lifestyles.

Birds who aspired to move up
in their organizations
were encouraged to become
as penguin-like as possible —
to shorten their steps
and learn the penguin stride,
to wear penguin suits,
and follow
the example of their leaders.

Employee Development Departments
offered
extensive training programs
on
appropriate penguin-like behavior.

The rules
and norms
were clear
from Day One.

Penguins advised in subtle
(and not so subtle) ways:

"This is the way we do things here."

"If you want to be successful,
be like us."

Some of the birds
who wanted to move up
in the pecking order
became very good
at taking on the penguin look
and penguin behaviors.

But even *they*
found that
they never quite
made it
into key positions.

It was assumed by all
that penguins
were natural leaders —
orderly, loyal, and good team players.

Penguins could be trusted
to put
the organization's interests
ahead
of personal and family concerns.

Other birds
were thought to be
more flighty
and less dependable.

Of course,
this was never stated
out loud
or in writing.

Because,
like every organization,
penguins wanted to be seen
as fair-minded and
ready to promote
on the basis of
talent,
hard work,
and contribution.

But everyone really knew —

The penguins
had always been in charge,
and
the penguins
would *always be in charge.*

The elder penguins
would take
younger penguins
under their wings
and coach them
on
how to be successful.

They would invite them
to play golf
and go jogging.

They would sit together
in the executive dining room
and talk about sports.

*It was clear to everyone
who the important penguins were.*

*It was also clear
that the penguins
felt most comfortable
around each other.*

Life was harmonious
in the Land of Penguins,
as long as everyone played
by the penguins' rules.

The other birds
in the organization
knew how to act
to make the penguins
feel comfortable
and secure.

But there came a time
when things began to change
in the Land of Penguins . . .

Senior penguins
would visit
other lands,
where they encountered
interesting birds
who impressed them
with their
management talent,
experience,
and accomplishments.

"These birds are not penguins,"
the elders thought,
"but perhaps
they could become penguins
if we brought them to our land
and trained them
in our penguin ways."

"Surely
these impressive and unusual birds
could adapt to life
in the Land of Penguins,
and the talent
they bring
would make us
even more successful."

"Our climate is different —
chilly and cold.
And our terrain is unique —
icy and barren.

"But we have thrived there
and so perhaps
will these new birds.

"If they are as smart
as we think they are,
they can adjust
to our weather and our ways."

And this was how
Perry the Peacock
came to live
in the Land of Penguins . . .

Now
Perry was clearly
not a penguin.

In fact,
he was the antithesis of penguinity —

Perry was a peacock —
a bright, colorful, and noisy bird.

Perry was a very talented peacock,
who had accomplished
some very impressive things
in his own land.

He could write well
and was excellent
at managing his budgets.
He was creative and imaginative,
and at the same time,
practical and sensible.

He had many friends and admirers
in his own land,
and was very popular and well-liked.

Senior managers
in the Land of Penguins
were intrigued
when they met Perry the Peacock.

They knew that he was different —
but they were impressed
with what he had achieved in his career,
and they were fascinated
with the possibilities
that he represented.

They felt that Perry
had real Penguin Potential.

Perry, in turn,
was attracted to the penguins
because of the great things
he had heard and read
about their land —
the promise of status,
and wealth,
and a sense of belonging
to a great and powerful enterprise.

It was a rich land —
and all the birds
were paid extremely well.

"My future will be brighter,"
he thought,
"in this new land."

And so the penguins
and the peacock
agreed.

He would join them,
and together
they would achieve
great things.

At first
everyone was delighted.

The penguins were pleased
and impressed
with their new recruit.

He stood out
from the crowd
in the way he sparkled
and displayed flashes of color
every now and then.

And Perry was pleased, too,
with the novelty
and the newness.

He was impressed
by the penguins —
they looked so important
in their black and white suits,
especially
when they gathered together
for meetings
and company events.

Their formality and manners
were so different
from anything
he had ever seen
or experienced
before.

Now the peacock
was careful
in the beginning
not to display
too much of his colorful nature.

You see, some friends
in his own land
had warned Perry about penguins —

They had cautioned him
about the rules
and the style
with which the penguins
governed their land.

So he kept his feathers
folded up
much of the time,
and would only occasionally
flash them open
to dazzle the penguins
with the full range of his talent and color.

He wanted
to be taken seriously
and he wanted
to be successful.

So he subdued
his own peacock nature
for a while,
until he could be sure
that the penguins had accepted him
completely.

He was confident
that when he produced
good results for them,
they would embrace him fully —
in all his peacock glory —
and he could relax
and just be himself.

You see,
things were very different
in the land where he had grown up —
in the Land of Learning.

In the Land of Learning
there were LOTS of different kinds of birds.

There were wise birds (owls),
and powerful birds (eagles),
and hunting birds (hawks),
improbable birds (ostriches),
elegant birds (swans),
and awkward birds (gooney birds).

It was crowded and noisy,
with a buzz of activity
and the rough and tumble
of competition.

Birds had to work hard,
learn fast,
and live by their wits
and creativity
in order to be successful.

It was an exhilarating
but tough
environment!

The motto in the Land of Learning was:

IMAGINE IT.
TRY IT.
PROVE IT.
DO IT!

All the birds
worked hard
to prove their talent
and earn their place
in the sun.

In the Land of Learning
the birds didn't always
get along peaceably.

Sometimes there were
conflicts and differences,
struggles and irritations.

But conflicts and differences
were valued
because the birds believed
that that's how new ideas get tested.

Discussion,
debate,
and argument —
that's the way
change was introduced
and progress was made.

Nobody cared
if you were a penguin or a peacock,
a dove or a bluejay.

Being smart
and talented
and productive
was all that mattered.

Initiative,
creativity,
and results
were most highly prized.

It was what was inside you
and what you contributed
that counted —
not the kind or color
of feathers you wore.

But Perry the Peacock
was in for
some very different challenges
when he left
the Land of Learning
and went to work
in the Land of Penguins.

He was used to hard work
and fighting for his ideas
and competing with
many different kinds of birds.
But nothing in his background
had prepared him for
the unique ways
and special customs
of the Land of Penguins.

He wanted to do well
and be successful.

He was flattered
that these powerful and prestigious penguins
had recruited him
into their ranks,
and he wanted to please them.

He studied the penguins' walk,
their talk,
and their style.

"How strange,"
he thought to himself,
"they all look alike.
They're like clones of each other."

He was intrigued
and puzzled
at the same time.

And as time went on, his troubles began . . .

Some of the penguins
   began to grumble
   that his distinctive peacock voice
   was too loud.

You see,
   penguins speak
   in very subdued,
   modulated
   tones,
   and the peacock's laughter
   and excited exclamations
   startled their time-honored
   sense of propriety.

His feathers began to show
more and more all the time,
as he worked hard
and accomplished
many great things.

Everyone agreed
that he was quite talented
and productive,
and they liked the impressive results
of his work.

But his flashy, colorful style
made some
of the senior penguins
uneasy.

Many of the other penguins
in the land
were delighted
with this new and unusual bird
in their midst.

They called him
"a breath of fresh air"
and welcomed his exuberance.

Some of the junior penguins
privately speculated
about how long he would last
in the Land of Penguins.
They saw
how un-penguinlike he was,
and wondered how long
this would be tolerated by the
elders.

A couple of the senior penguins
tried to take him
under their wings and coach him.

"Look," they said,
"we like your work,
   but some of the elders
   are uncomfortable with your style."

"You need to change to be accepted here."

"Why don't you put on a penguin suit,
   so you look more like us?"

"It doesn't fit,"
responded Perry the Peacock.

"It's too tight and constraining.
My tail feathers will get crushed
and my wings can't move well."

"I can't work if I'm not comfortable."

The elders said,
"Well then,
maybe you could paint your feathers
black and white,
like ours."

"Then at least
you wouldn't look
quite so different."

"What's wrong with the way I am?"
Perry asked.

He was hurt and confused.

"I work hard,
I produce great results —
everyone says so."

"Why can't you look at my work
rather than my feathers?"

"Aren't my accomplishments
more important
than my style?"

"It's such a small thing,"
the penguins responded.

"You are smart and talented.
You could have a bright future here.
You just need to act
more like us
and then
the elders will be more comfortable."

"You need to wear a penguin suit,
and soften your voice,
and shorten your steps."

"Just watch all the other penguins —
see how they act?"

"Try to be like the rest of us."

Perry believed
that their intentions were good,
but their words wounded him nonetheless.

"Why can't I just be who I am?
Why do I have to change
to be accepted by you?"
he asked.

"That's just the way things are here,"
the penguins shrugged.

"It's the same everywhere
in the Sea of Organizations."

He suspected they might be right,
but his heart didn't want to accept it.

He thanked them
for their words of advice
and their concern for him,
and he went back to his nest
to think things over.

As the months rolled by,
he discussed his dilemma
with some of the other birds he trusted.

Several of them
were also new birds
who had been recruited
around the same time as
Perry's arrival
in the Land of Penguins.

Many of them
were experiencing
similar kinds
of problems . . .

Edward the Eagle
complained that he, too,
was getting pressure
to change.

He was smart and powerful
and very skilled at his work,
and he even wore the requisite penguin suit.

But Edward didn't talk
or act like a penguin,
and this bothered the elders.

They were embarrassed
by his accent,
and sent him to
a prestigious,
tradition-steeped
Eastern Business School
for special executive penguin training.

But it didn't work —
he was still an eagle in penguin's clothing.

He couldn't change who he was.

And Helen the Hawk
had similar problems.

She was beautiful and powerful —
smart, sharp, and aggressive.
She was a skilled hunter,
with fierce competitive instincts.

She wore her penguin suit,
occasionally more colorful
than the male penguins,
but still acceptable.

Helen tried to adapt
to the style of the penguins,
but her hawk-like nature
would always reveal itself.

Her talons were sharp,
her eyes piercing,
her manner intense,
her hunter's instincts
ever alert.

And her aggressive style
made the elders very uncomfortable.

It was the same story
with Mike the Mockingbird.

He was an especially brilliant bird —
creative,
imaginative,
and impulsive.
He was attracted by sparkling ideas.

He flew fast,
worked hard,
and jumped around
making good things happen
all over the Land of Penguins.

But Mike soon discovered that
penguins are territorial birds,
who build their empires,
establish their pecking order,
and fiercely resent anyone
who comes into their turf
without being properly invited.

Since Mike was not a penguin,
he was not sensitive
to the politics
and the turf issues
of the senior penguins.

With his penchant for creativity
and imagining possibilities
outside the ordinary,
he sometimes offended
some of the elders
by flying into their territories.

They were threatened and annoyed
at his intrusions.

Like Edward the Eagle
and Helen the Hawk,
Mike wore his penguin suit
and tried his best
to learn the ways of the penguins
so he would be accepted by them.

But ultimately,
he could not change who he really was.

The story was similar
with Sara the Swan.

She was an optimistic dreamer,
with unusual visions
for the future
of the Land of Penguins.

She had interesting ideas,
unique ideas,
good ideas —

but her ideas
often were not heard
because she expressed them
in such a gentle way.

Her style was graceful,
her manner gracious,
but the penguins
had doubts about
her toughness
and her strength.

There were others as well . . .

The thing they all had in common
was that none of them
had grown up
in the Land of Penguins.

They had been
recruited and hired
from other places.

The penguin elders
had enticed these outsiders
with promises of success:

"We want your fresh thinking
and new ideas.
We admire your track record
and want you to do
great things for us."

But
as soon as the new birds
were inside the organization,
the elders issued them
penguin suits
and began pressuring them
to talk,
act,
and think
more like penguins.

The penguins said,
"We value diversity."

But their actions said otherwise.

As the exotic new birds
discussed
their mutual frustrations
among themselves,
they tried
to figure out
what to do.

Several of them
decided to try
to change the culture
rather than
let the culture change them.

"We'll work on our bosses,
and other key penguins,"
they vowed,
"without
being too obvious,
of course."

They each
developed strategies
for becoming
Agents of Change
within the Land of Penguins.

Edward the Eagle
adopted a **"Strategy of Support."**

> *"Catch your boss*
> *doing something right . . .*
> *(or approximately right!)"*

Whenever his boss
accepted
any new idea,
Edward would reinforce him
by saying,
"I appreciate
your willingness
to try
something different.
Your support
makes my job
interesting
and rewarding."

Helen the Hawk
had her own ideas
about how to bring about change.
She used a **"Strategy of Hopeful Thinking."**

*"Act on the basis
of assumptions
you'd like to be true . . .
(with caution, of course!)"*

Helen would regularly send
her boss
newspaper clippings
and magazine articles
with a personal note
which read:

"Because
of your continuing interest
in learning new ways
to handle our marketing,
I thought
you'd like to see
the attached article
about
Prosperous Enterprise, Inc.
in the recent issue of
the 'Journal of Successful **Organizations.'"**

Mike the Mockingbird
decided he would try
an extremely bold strategy —
a **"Strategy of Calculated Ignorance."**

"Violate

penguin policy —

and if caught —

use the Puzzled Prodigal Response."

Whenever Mike was questioned
about making a particular decision,
he would assume
an expression of puzzlement
as he described
how a shortcut
would achieve something
that everyone
had agreed
was important.

Sara the Swan,
being much gentler
in her approach,
tried a *"Strategy of Safe Learning."*

> *"Expose*
> *the Senior Penguins*
> *to new ideas*
> *in settings*
> *where*
> *they won't be embarrassed*
> *by having to respond."*

Sara would casually mention
her ideas and suggestions
in quiet conversations
and informal settings.

She "planted ideas,"
nurtured them slowly,
and watched for progress.

Some of the other birds —
who were determined
to transform themselves —
tried very hard
to become penguins.

They walked the penguin walk;
they talked the penguin talk.

They preened
and practiced
to produce the desired result.

But ultimately they failed,
because
they couldn't change
who they really were.

And a few birds,
like Perry,
didn't even try
to become penguins.

Perry just knew
in his heart
that there must be
at least *one* land in
the vast Sea of Organizations
where
he could be a peacock
and be valued
for his uniqueness.

He resisted
the penguins' advice and pressure,
firm in his conviction
that he should be valued
for his results.

Over time,
things got worse
for Perry
and the other exotic birds
in the Land of Penguins . . .

Their strategies
to change
the penguin way of doing things
met with
resistance and red tape.

Their ideas and efforts
were discounted
and dismissed.

Their questions of "Why?"
were answered with:
"This is the way
we've *always* done things here."

The exotic birds learned
through painful experience
that the culture
of the land
was deeply entrenched.

The structures and systems
were rigid and unbending.
Policies and procedures
ensured the continuity
of the penguin practices.

It eventually became clear
that individual efforts
at persuasion and influence
were foolish and futile
in the face of such
longstanding tradition
and structure.

The exotic birds realized
that the penguin ways
had developed
over many years
and would not change
easily or soon.

Their strategies
to change themselves
also fell short,
because
deep down inside
they just weren't penguins.

*They couldn't change
who they really were.*

Their hearts were filled
with frustration,
disappointment,
and sadness.

They had come
to the Land of Penguins
with such high hopes
and great expectations.

They had wanted to contribute
and be successful.

*But what they got instead
was quiet criticism,
stifling conformity,
and subtle rejection.*

And so,
one by one,
Perry and the other new birds
each began to realize
the same thing —

*They could not be themselves
in the Land of Penguins.*

They had to move on.

They knew their futures
lay somewhere else
in the vast Sea of Organizations.

Some of the new birds
left the Land of Penguins
on their own.

Others
were pushed out
by the senior penguins,
who said,
"You make us too uncomfortable.
You don't fit here.
You must leave."

Whether they left on their own
or were forced out by the elders,
all the departing birds
shared one thing in common —
the pain and confusion
of being different,
and the sadness
and disappointment
of not being accepted for who they were.

These birds of a different feather
had all struggled
with the same dilemma:

How much
could they
or would they
change to "fit in"
and be accepted
in the Land of Penguins,
and how much
could they be themselves?

What price would they pay to be successful?

And the penguins had their own dilemma:

How much diversity
could they tolerate in their land
and still maintain
their own comfort level?

Wouldn't
all these differences
endanger
their harmonious corporate culture?

The penguins,
after all,
had enjoyed
many years of profitable success
by following
historic penguin traditions
and ways of doing business.

They were reluctant
to change the style
that had made them great.

And they were disappointed
that so many
of their new recruits
did not work out.

Perry the Peacock
was the first to leave.

He had many friends
from other lands,
and they told him
of a new and wondrous place
they had visited in their travels.

They described it as
"the Land of Opportunity."

There,
they told him,
his work
and his contributions
would be valued —
and his uniqueness
would be applauded,
not criticized.

He could be
colorful,
flamboyant,
and enthusiastic,
and others would appreciate him
for his distinctive style.

Dare he hope
that these reports were true?

Was this the place
he had longed for?

He had to go
and see for himself.

When Perry arrived in
the Land of Opportunity
he found that it
was totally different
from the Land of Penguins . . .

Here,
workers and bosses
didn't waste
time and energy
pretending to be
something different
from what they were.

They knew
that they needed
many different kinds of birds
in order to thrive
in the turbulent and competitive
Sea of Organizations.

And they knew that
the most important requirement
for organizational success
is acceptance and trust.

It is acceptance and trust
that make it possible
for each bird
to sing its own song —
confident that it will be heard —
even by those
who sing with a different voice.

All the birds
expressed themselves freely,
and their lively exchanges
of differing views
ensured
that their work
and their ways
were constantly improving.

Best of all,
they had confidence
in their leaders,
birds of many kinds
who had risen to
their positions
through talent,
skill,
and ability.

The motto here was:

Some birds swam,
many flew,
and some kept their feet
planted firmly on the ground.

This gave them
many different perspectives
on the world —
which they shared
easily and openly
with one another.

Their shared knowledge made them wise.
And their wisdom made them successful.

Perry knew
he had found his new home.

As the months and years
rolled by,
one by one,
Edward the Eagle,
Helen the Hawk,
Mike the Mockingbird,
and Sara the Swan
also made their way
to the Land of Opportunity.

They had heard from Perry
about the freedom
and openness
that existed there.

In this land,
Edward could fly free and high,
soaring as fast
as his wings could carry him.

Others admired
his grace and power —
and commented
on what an inspiration he was
to younger birds
who came from humble beginnings
but had ambitious dreams
of flying high someday themselves.

Nobody even noticed
the way he spoke,
with his unique accent.

Helen,
who had rattled the penguins
with her intensity
and her keen competitive instincts,
found a place
where she was welcome
in the Land of Opportunity.

Her colleagues
valued her hunting skills
and her ability to spot
changing trends
and possibilities
for new ventures.

They commented frequently
on her elegant beauty
and distinctive style.

She was perfectly suited
for her new position
in the Land of Opportunity.

Mike
at long last
experienced the creative joy
of jumping from project to project,
working hard and fast,
and stirring up new ideas
wherever he went.

No longer fettered
by a rigid pecking order
and boundaries
dictated by penguins,
his productivity skyrocketed —
and others marveled
at his amazing skills.

Sara, too,
found the Land of Opportunity
to be a hospitable place
for her dreamy,
reflective,
imaginative
style of working.

She started writing
and pursuing ideas
in ways
she once thought
would never be possible
in a place of work.

Other birds flocked to her,
wanting to work with her
and share
in the realization
of her dreams.

She was appreciated
for the freedom
she allowed others,
and
for her gentle style.

These diverse birds
all prospered and grew
as never before.

They felt affirmed
and appreciated
by the other birds
in the land.

They experienced a new freedom,
allowing them to fly,
each with their own unique style.

They worked hard —
and enjoyed
the fruits of their labors.

*A*bove all else,
they knew the joy of just being themselves.

Perry the Peacock flashed his colorful feathers;

Edward the Eagle soared with power and grace;

Helen the Hawk skillfully kept watch and hunted;

Mike the Mockingbird followed his creative instincts and innovative ideas; and

Sara the Swan drifted and floated with the currents.

Perry and his friends
found that
life was good and
their future was bright
in the Land of Opportunity.

There
they could all succeed —
each with a different style —
and make contributions
that would be welcomed and appreciated
by their colleagues
and coworkers.

*They came to realize
that the Land of Opportunity
is more than a place . . .*

It is a state of mind.

The Land of Opportunity is an attitude.

It is
an openness to new ideas,
a willingness to listen,
an eagerness to learn,
a desire to grow,
and the flexibility to change.

The Land of Opportunity
is a new way of dealing with one another.

It becomes a reality
when we stop judging each other
by superficial criteria
and begin to see
and appreciate
everyone
as uniquely
talented,
capable,
and valuable.

The Land of Opportunity
is where we live and work
when we choose
to see with new eyes,
live from our hearts,
and allow ourselves
and others
to be what we truly are . . .

Ourselves.

The End

Afterword

. . . and what of the Land of Penguins?

Their story continues to unfold every day
in corporations and organizations
across the country . . .

Part II

Tips and Tools
for Feathered Friends

For peacocks and other exotic birds
who are trying to find the way
to their own Land of Opportunity...

Are You a Peacock
(or Other Type of Exotic Bird)?

YES NO

☐ ☐ 1. Do you frequently feel like you don't fit in — that you are *different* in some fundamental way?

☐ ☐ 2. Do you get criticized for not being a "team player" ("Team player" = a euphemism for conforming to group norms.)

☐ ☐ 3. Do you feel pressured by your boss or others to change in some significant way to fit in?

☐ ☐ 4. Do you feel ostracized, lonely, left out of the loop of information and decision-making?

☐ ☐ 5. Are you unable to identify with anyone as a role model at the top of your organization?

☐ ☐ 6. Are your ideas and suggestions routinely rejected as "not the way we do things here"?

☐ ☐ 7. Do you often feel under- or unappreciated for your talent and skill, while others who are less talented get promoted and rewarded?

☐ ☐ 8. Do you often try to figure out "what's wrong with me"?

☐ ☐ 9. Do you feel stifled, stuck, frustrated by some unseen "system"?

☐ ☐ 10. Are you frequently ignored, interrupted, or discounted when you make comments or suggestions at meetings?

══ ══   Totals

If you answered "yes" to six or more of these questions, you are definitely a peacock or some other type of exotic bird in your organization!

If you answered "yes" to four or five of these questions, you are probably somewhat ambivalent about where you are working. In some ways you fit, and in other ways you struggle.

If you answered "yes" to three or fewer questions, you might be an exotic bird in the Land of Opportunity, or you might be a penguin in the Land of Penguins. The point is, you are probably a pretty good fit in your organization.

Survival Strategies for Peacocks
Who Want to Stay Put

1. Don't let your work suffer because you're discouraged about being different. Strive for excellence in all you do. Your professional track record is your most important asset, both inside the Land of Penguins and outside.

2. Seek out other exotic birds (both inside and outside your organization) for friendship, networking, and moral support.

3. Make conscious and careful choices about how much you can and will adapt or change to be successful in the penguins' eyes. What price are you willing to pay? (See "Strategies for Birds of Different Feathers.")

4. Be prepared and flexible enough to put on a penguin suit occasionally when it's necessary and/or important. Think of it as "penguin camouflage."

5. Know that you are not defective — there is nothing wrong with you. Your talent, skill, and ideas are valuable, even if the penguins don't recognize or reward you.

Tips for Peacocks
Who Want to Fly the Coop

1. Be realistic about the world of work. You're going to find *some* penguins in most organizations, especially the large ones.

2. Try to stay out of organizations that are heavily dominated by penguins. If you're still working in one, keep your eyes open for more innovation-friendly places to work (especially small, entrepreneurial organizations).

3. Consider self-employment as an option. It's not for everyone, but many exotic birds are living happier lives by opting out of mainstream organizations.

4. Take comfort in the fact that you are not alone. There are many, many peacocks and exotic birds who feel the same way you do. Seek them out; ask their advice; take heart in their successes.

5. Be a good example to other exotic birds. Be supportive, help other birds, encourage those who are different to find their way to happiness and success.

Strategies for
Birds of Different Feathers

If you are a peacock or some other exotic bird in your organization, you have options and choices about whether you should stay there or fly the coop to another job in another organization, or to self-employment.

If you stay, then you have many choices about how best to survive (maybe even thrive!) in a less-than-perfect work environment. Each of the strategies described here has its pros and cons. A few of these strategies will seem realistic and do-able in your situation. Some may seem inauthentic or distasteful to you. Others may appeal to you, but you're not sure you can carry them off. Still others may be politically dangerous in your organization, or may jeopardize your long-term career goals.

Discuss these strategies with friends you trust. Evaluate them in light of your own personal situation before you decide which strategies to adopt. Only *you* can decide what's appropriate for you and your career future. Perhaps this list of strategies will stimulate your own creativity as you plan your future — inside or outside the Land of Penguins.

BLUEBIRD STRATEGY — Stay cheerful. Try to make the best of a difficult situation. You may be the kind of person who can put a positive spin on any situation. You are probably an optimist by nature, and you often see the good in other people, and you see the silver lining in every cloud. This strategy can be quite effective, because you often get what you expect in terms of positive outcomes, and even when you don't, you know how to turn lemons into lemonade!

PARROT STRATEGY — Mimic those around you. Work hard to be as much like them as you can so you'll fit in. People who adopt this strategy are good at assimilating into an organization — they are flexible and adaptable and can often fit in very well. This is a fine strategy and can lead to great career success. However, parrots need to be aware that the personal price they pay for adapting may be very high. Some people almost lead double lives — they act one way at work, and they can only relax and be themselves away from work. Think twice before you sell your soul to be successful.

SPARROW STRATEGY — Be neutral and try to blend into the background. Keep a low profile and nobody will notice you. This strategy can help you to survive for a long time, and you may be happy flying through your career like this. You will probably survive many organizational dangers and threats. Since you don't stand out, you probably will not be a target. But you may pay a price by never experiencing the exhilaration of contributing new ideas, taking risks, taking a stand on an important issue on which you have strong feelings, or gaining credibility and visibility for potential career advancement.

HUMMINGBIRD STRATEGY — Move fast; be efficient. (It's hard to hit a moving target.) You can get a lot of mileage out of this strategy, and be quite successful in your organization and your career. You will probably be seen as a good worker who can be depended upon to produce quick results.

CANARY STRATEGY — Be colorful and charming; fit in by becoming the center of positive attention. Being charming and entertaining can take you a long way in life and in your work — especially in certain fields. This is a natural strategy for people in sales and marketing, public relations, and human resources, and it can be equally effective in many other fields as well. But be careful that you develop some substance to back up that style. If you're all fluff, people will figure that out sooner or later.

SWAN STRATEGY — Do your job and gain respect by being dignified. Some people command the respect of others by virtue of their impressive personal presence. They convey an image of natural poise and confidence. This often comes from a deep-seated sense of self-worth or demonstrated competence and skill. Swans can be very successful in their careers and in their lives.

VULTURE STRATEGY — Shrug off your differentness. Make yourself indispensable by doing the jobs nobody else wants to do. Every organization needs scavengers — people who will do the jobs that everyone else dislikes. You may take on the "mission impossible" projects that others are afraid to tackle; or you may willingly do the boring but important work that needs to get done. You can make yourself a key player in your organization by using this vulture strategy.

OWL STRATEGY — Become valuable and important to the organization by becoming an expert at something the organization needs. Every organization needs owls — technical specialists, subject-matter experts, or simply thoughtful old-timers who have a lot of organizational history and learning in their heads. You can make yourself an indispensable part of your group if you become an owl.

HAWK STRATEGY — Become valuable to the organization by being a skilled hunter — bringing in new business, new opportunities. Hawks are very valuable in any organization, and they are usually appreciated and treated very well, even if they are somewhat different from the mainstream. Your job security and your career success are a function of your ability to generate opportunities, new business, or growth in the organization. You'll do well.

DOVE STRATEGY — Become the peacemaker, the troubleshooter who solves problems. This is an important role, since all organizations experience conflicts or problems — in operations, in employee relations, in finance, in marketing, and in many other areas of work. If you are good at resolving conflicts, sorting out complex issues, and solving problems, you will be valued by your organization — by *any* organization!

EAGLE STRATEGY — Rise above the situation and play a leadership role in changing your organization for the better. It's not easy being an eagle. It often means ignoring your own feelings for the sake of a larger good, and making personal sacrifices that will benefit everyone in the long run. There is always a price for becoming a leader, but there are also great rewards. Do you want to be a leader in your organization? Can you make a contribution that will help create a better workplace with a strong future? If so, soar as fast and as high as your wings will carry you. The world needs more leaders!

PEACOCK STRATEGY — Dazzle others with your incredible talent and positive results. But be aware that others may be uncomfortable with your flash and dazzle, or they may be threatened by your success. Peacocks can be quite successful as superstars in any field, but it can sometimes backfire on them when other people are put off by their style. You may have to learn when to keep your feathers folded up modestly and when it's OK to flash them open for effect. Most people enjoy being around peacocks, but sometimes peacocks overdo a good thing (and it can turn into a bit of a problem). Some organizations (like penguin organizations) will not tolerate peacock behavior at all, so peacocks should be careful about where they decide to work and realize that they may be required to change their behavior when they work there.

OSTRICH STRATEGY — Bury your head in the sand. Pretend nothing is wrong. This strategy may work for you for a while, but in the long run it will probably not serve you well. Ignoring organizational realities can endanger your career potential and leave you open to getting blindsided when you least expect it.

CHICKEN STRATEGY — Cower and complain about how awful things are, but don't venture forth to try to change things. You can see that there are problems in your organization — problems that have a negative impact on you. But you are too frightened or too insecure to take a risk to try to change things. This strategy may keep you safe, but it will also add to your feelings of powerlessness and insignificance.

GOOSE STRATEGY — Cut your losses and fly south in search of a more hospitable environment. Sometimes what's important is to know when to cut your losses and move on. If there are irreconcilable differences between you and your organization (or you and your boss), and none of the other strategies seem workable to you, then leaving the organization might be your best option. This is a highly personal decision, and only you can decide if it's the right choice for you.

OTHER STRATEGIES — Be creative and write your own!

_____

_____

_____

_____

_____

Positive Penguinship: What Peacocks Can Learn from Penguins

It's easy to get annoyed with penguins — especially if you're a peacock. Penguins are set in their ways, and can be arrogant and pompous. But it's well to remember that most penguins have good intentions. They may be stuck in their ways and narrow-minded, but that doesn't mean they are completely useless to the organization. While you don't want your organization to be dominated by shortsighted-ness and bureaucratic inertia, there might be a few things we can learn from our interactions with penguins. Here are a few possibilities:

1. Sometimes it is best to err on the side of caution when evaluating new ideas and proposed projects. Following one's creative instincts is good, but occa-sionally taking a penguin perspective can help keep us from being too impulsive. We can learn to take *calcu-lated* risks, not foolish ones.

2. Because there are many penguins in power in organi-zations of all types and sizes, it is important to be able to relate to them effectively. You would do well to keep a penguin suit handy and learn "penguin speak" so that you can interact with and influence powerful penguins when you need to. Consider it an exercise in flexibility. The better you are at relating to penguins (and all types of birds), the more successful you'll be.

3. Most penguins are the way they are because being penguins made them successful in the past. What can you learn from this? What attitudes and behaviors have made *you* successful in the past? Will the same things make you successful in the future, or do you need to expand your repertoire? Are there any penguin traits that might be helpful for you to learn?

4. Are there certain jobs or fields for which penguins are especially well suited? You need some measure of tradition, institutional memory, and focus on detail in every organization. Put penguins in positions where they can do what they do best. Play to their strengths, so they can contribute to your organization's success.

There's a Little Bit of Penguin in All of Us

The penguin metaphor we use in our story refers to anyone who is narrow-minded, tradition-bound, risk-averse, conservative, resistant to new ideas or different perspectives, and tied to the way he or she has always done things. Penguins may or may not be managers or executives. Penguins can be found at any level in an organization. Remember, being a penguin is a mind-set, an attitude, a characteristic way of looking at the world.

If we really look carefully and honestly, we'll probably find a little bit of penguin in ourselves, too — though we may not want to admit it. Even the staunchest peacock probably has a little penguin streak somewhere deep inside. Most of us have an aspect of our lives in which we too are narrow-minded, stuck in our ways, resistant to new approaches. We are creatures of habit, with familiar routines we don't want to change.

- "I always take this route to work."

- "This is where I always sit at staff meetings."

- "The end of the toilet paper should always go *over* the roll, not under."

- "The drinking glasses in the kitchen cabinet should go upside down, not right side up. Everyone knows that."

Quack, quack, quack. Listen to ourselves resisting different ways of doing things. There really *is* a little penguin in all of us.

That's not a bad thing, it's a normal thing. What's important here is to simply recognize these penguin tendencies when they show up so that they don't control you. You want to be able to let go of your penguin streak when it doesn't serve you — when it keeps you from being flexible and adaptable to change, or when it keeps you from taking appropriate risks and trying new things. (Consider asking someone you trust and respect to alert you whenever you start acting this way.)

What you most want to avoid is having your little penguin tendencies grow to take over your whole personality. If you become a total penguin, you become a problem — for yourself and for others.

How can you tell if you're becoming a complete penguin? Listen to yourself speak; check out the list in "Recognizing the Quack" in Part III on page 128 and see how often you say those things. Pay attention to how you respond to other people who have different opinions from yours:

- Do you bristle?

- Do you automatically resist suggestions that don't fit with the way you like to do things?

- Do you resent changes that are out of your control?

- Do you keep doing things *your* way, even if someone shows you a better way?

If you found yourself answering "yes" to more than one of these questions, you just might be turning into one of those black-and-white birds. Talks like a penguin, thinks like a penguin, waddles like a penguin... must be a penguin!

Quick! Read the next section.... Help is on the way!

Part III

Ideas and Examples
for Teaching Penguins to Fly

How You Can Tell If You Work in the Land of Penguins

1. Decision-making emphasizes precedent, tradition, and control ("That's never been done before" or "That's against company policy") — rather than creativity, risk-taking, flexibility, and innovation ("Seems like a good idea — let's try it").

2. Excessive emphasis is placed on "chain of command" and "not rocking the boat." Loyalty to your boss (or other powerful people) is valued over loyalty to the organization or the customer.

3. Discussions are characterized by group-think — with little disagreement or debate. Avoidance of confrontation or clash with tradition and the existing order.

4. It is extremely important to publicly adhere to the "company line" and be discreet in all conversations. You must be careful whom you trust with your candid opinions, and *never* point out that "the Emperor Penguin has no clothes."

5. "Organizational constipation" makes *everything* move slowly. Very bureaucratic — several layers of approval are required to launch new projects, resolve customer problems, make purchases, and so on.

6. Problem-solving is subject to "analysis paralysis" — too many committees that study issues but have no authority to make decisions; low level of risk-taking.

7. The organization tends to add layers of management rather than eliminate them. Special jobs are created for the "fair-haired boys" (and girls) as grooming positions. Up-and-coming fast-trackers are simply younger versions of those already in power.

8. People refer to "the good ol' boy system" as the way things get done and people get ahead. Promotions and plum assignments are based more on "who you know" and being one of "the chosen ones" than on skill and ability.

9. Newcomers are encouraged to assimilate, conform, fit in. Form is valued over content. Compatible style is often more important than results. Failure to fit in has dire consequences for one's career.

10. The top executives look like they all go to the same tailor and the same barber. Conservative bias in attire, thinking, and behavior.

11. Trappings of status and power are visible and prominent (i.e., executive dining rooms, executive cars, executive bathrooms, and so on). Excessive emphasis on rank and position power within the organization.

12. Few women and ethnic minorities are in leadership positions. Those who *are* there are often the staunchest penguins of all, to prove their loyalty to the existing order.

Recognizing the "Quack"
(Common Phrases from Penguins)

- "That's not the way we do things here."
- "We've always done it this way."
- "If it ain't broke, don't fix it."
- "Keep your mouth shut. Just be glad you've got a job."
- "It can't happen here."
- "It can't be done."
- "Senior management will never go for that."
- "Don't violate the chain of command."
- "Don't rock the boat."
- "The boss doesn't like bad news."
- "Let's play it safe on this..."
- "People will think you're crazy if you suggest that."
- "That's not your job. Leave that kind of thing up to _____ (other department)."
- "We're in retrenchment mode. Not a good time to try something new and risky."
- "C.Y.A." (Cover Your A- . . . er, uh, tail feathers!)
- "It's *my* way or the highway."

Tips for Penguins Who Want to Change Themselves

1. Look at your own biases and attitudes — acknowledge them honestly to yourself and stay aware of them. Consciousness is the first step toward change.

2. Practice divergent thinking — there are many paths to success and many different ways to do things and accomplish results. Your way is only one way. Applaud creativity, innovation, and resourcefulness in others.

3. Try to separate style from substance. Don't get hung up on stylistic differences with others — keep your focus on substance, shared goals and objectives, and results.

4. Get out of your comfort zone. Go out of your way to spend time with people who are different from you. Invite an exotic bird to lunch, or to other business/social events.

5. Be a visible role model to other penguins. People watch what you *do* more than what you *say*. Incorporate exotic birds into your daily interactions and activities. Consider mentoring exotic birds, while allowing them to be themselves.

Tips for Penguins Who Want to Change Their Organizations

1. Recognize that the world is changing and the future looks very different from the past. What worked in the past may now be obsolete. A new future requires new ideas and perspectives.

2. Create opportunities for exotic birds to contribute their talents and ideas — project teams, task forces, special projects.

3. Continually reevaluate work processes, policies, and procedures. Don't assume that the "tried and true" will continue to work indefinitely. A product, a service, a work process can become obsolete overnight, and you may find yourself *behind* the curve instead of ahead of it. Constant vigilance and continual reevaluation are the watchwords of the day.

4. Provide processes and people to help birds of *all* kinds deal with their feelings about change and your organization's future. Make it safe to talk about fears and anxieties, hopes and aspirations.

5. Celebrate small successes — both individual and organizational. Change is bumpy and uncomfortable. Reward the progress your organization makes. Keep up your commitment to new thinking and innovation!

Preventing
Penguin Paralysis

- Try holding stand-up meetings instead of sit-down meetings. This technique tends to speed up discussion and decision-making. The meeting can't go on too long if everyone is standing.

- Try lots of experiments. Experiments are trial balloons, short-term pilot projects, and such. They will encourage innovation and reasonable risk-taking, without requiring a wholesale commitment to a new idea. Budget for the experiments as a regular business expense. Allow for the fact that many experiments will fail; this is part of the normal price of innovation.

- Timing is everything. Allow enough time for brainstorming and discussion, but also set tight timelines for decision-making. Don't keep waiting for more data; you'll never have *all* the data you'd like. Learn when it's time to go with what you have.

- Hire innovative, creative people and then let them innovate — even though it shakes up the established order. If you don't trust their judgment, then don't hire them in the first place.

- If you haven't done so already, flatten your organization and get rid of layers in the approval process for new ideas.

The Care and Feeding of Peacocks:
A Penguin's Guide

Peter Drucker, probably the most respected of all management consultants, says that organizations need two kinds of people — they need bureaucrats... and they need lunatics! Bureaucrats keep the system running in an orderly fashion, while lunatics challenge the system with innovation and new ideas.

We call them penguins and peacocks. We need some penguins in our organizations as a conservative force, to maintain tradition, to provide institutional memory and keep us from repeating the past, and to provide some stability in the face of constant change. Penguins make sure that all the i's are dotted and the t's are crossed.

At the same time, we need peacocks in our organizations to provide creativity and new thinking. Innovation and breakthroughs almost never come from the penguins — breakthroughs always come from the peacocks, those outside the mainstream. Peacocks and other exotic birds are the ones who see things from different perspectives, who are always looking for the new angle, and they are outside the mainstream of tradition and predictability.

For penguins, the challenge is this: to realize that the odd bird in your department or organization who annoys you the most is probably the one you *need* the most! That crazy bird is the one who is going to keep questioning the tried and true, and is the one who comes up with so many oddball projects and schemes. But that crazy bird is also the one who is most likely to have the next million-dollar idea. So the question is: Have you hugged your peacocks lately? How can you feed and nurture these colorful (but sometimes annoying) birds so that they can contribute their brilliance to your organization's success? Here are a few suggestions:

- Peacocks and other exotic birds need a lot of freedom. Do not frustrate them with bureaucratic red tape and micromanagement. You'll drive them crazy, or you'll drive them away. Create a working environment that allows them lots of autonomy and flexibility. Turn them loose to do what they do best.

- Focus on the contributions your peacocks make, and learn to ignore or overlook their eccentricities. As one manager summarized, "You gotta make allowances for genius." Be flexible, and develop a tolerance for off-the-wall behavior. It's results that count; as long as your peacocks are producing results for you, don't sweat the small stuff.

- Let your peacocks know how much you value them. They generally need a lot of appreciation and recognition. Let them flash their colorful feathers often. Tell them they are brilliant and beautiful.

- Create a work environment where all types of birds can flourish — peacocks, owls, doves, swans, hawks, and others. Show appreciation for the many different kinds of contributions they make. Play to their strengths. Don't try to make one type of bird into another. Let them be themselves, and let them know they are valued as unique individuals.

- Provide team training that teaches everyone how to work effectively with others who are different from themselves. We all tend to think our own style is the best, and we can be critical of others who differ from us. Frequent training and ongoing conversations about the value of differences will help keep everyone aware that it would be a boring world, indeed, if we were all alike. *Vive la différence!*

Reports from the Field

What influence have Perry the Peacock and his colorful friends had on the individuals in organizations who have read the story? Are corporations becoming less penguin-like? Are bureaucracies losing their stultifying grip on employee initiative and innovation? Are "birds of different feathers" finding their organizations more receptive to alternative points of view and new ideas?

We wanted to find out, so we asked some of the people who have been using *A Peacock in the Land of Penguins.* We discovered that the story is being adopted in a variety of ways in different kinds of organizations:

- New-employee orientation
- Team-building training
- Management and leadership training
- Strategic-planning retreats
- Community-outreach efforts
- Diversity seminars
- Internet-based training

Penguins in organizations both large and small are "learning to fly" — they are getting out of their penguin suits and trying new behaviors.

- For some penguins, learning to fly means getting out of their comfort zones and spending time with people who are very different from themselves.

- For other penguins, learning to fly means saying "yes" to new ideas when their knee-jerk response in the past has always been "no."

- And for still others, learning to fly means working more effectively in teams, listening to and learning from those who may have some pretty far-out ideas.

For all these penguins, learning to fly requires both courage and humility, to admit that tried-and-true answers from the past may not be appropriate anymore. Learning to fly means feeling awkward sometimes, and the penguins are good sports about the clumsiness that is part and parcel of learning new behaviors.

The following pages are reports from the field — works in progress, as various organizations try their hand at teaching penguins to fly. They are to be applauded for their openness to change and their willingness to share their stories with our readers.

John Deere Credit Canada

"Canada needs to bring out the best in its employees," this company told us. "We need to focus on the diversity of ideas and thinking. How do we leverage the brainpower and creativity of all our different employees across Canada? This is a competitiveness issue for us; how do we tap into the creativity of diversity so that we maintain our leadership in a highly competitive business?"

They decided to custom-design a one-day seminar for all their employees, using the story of Perry the Peacock to stimulate their own thinking about innovation and new ideas. Some of the questions JDCC wrestled with during the seminars:

• What are some of our assumptions and blind spots that get in the way of embracing new ideas?

• How have we been hampered by "business as usual" thinking?

• How can we encourage innovation and initiative in sales, in financing, in marketing, in every aspect of our company?

• What can we start doing differently that will encourage the peacocks in our company to stay with JDCC and contribute their ideas?

• What policies and procedures do we need to change to be faster and more flexible?

- What can the senior-management team do to create a culture of innovation and risk-taking?

- How can we stay ahead of the curve in our business?

Of course, those seminars were just the beginning for John Deere Credit Canada. The dialogue started in those sessions but continues today, in staff meetings, at sales conferences, and in day-to-day interaction among JDCC employees.

IBM Australia/New Zealand

Many people think of IBM as the ultimate penguin company. Renowned for their navy blue suits, white shirts, and ties, the IBM penguins have valued their proud tradition of excellence and professionalism.

So when IBMers say they want to learn how to break out of their penguin suits, you know that something significant is afoot in the corporate world. The IBM executives in Australia and New Zealand embraced the story of Perry the Peacock and bought copies of the book for all their associates. They designed training programs to cultivate a new atmosphere of innovation and risk-taking. They rewarded their salespeople for creative new approaches to getting and keeping profitable customers. They knew that they were no longer in the business of delivering big boxes of computer equipment — they were now in the business of delivering business solutions to their customers.

Do they still have a ways to go? Sure. You don't change decades of penguin behavior overnight. But the IBM penguins "down under" are flapping their wings as fast as they can, determined to become airborne in the brave new world of technology in the 21st century.

Kellogg

Kellogg uses *A Peacock in the Land of Penguins* in three interesting ways:

First, Kellogg sees the *Peacock* tale as a wonderful way to get new employees off to a great start, by using it in their new-employee orientation program, "Foundations." Perry the Peacock's story is a simple but powerful way of letting new hires know from Day One that their wide variety of talents and ideas are important to the company. Participants are encouraged to think about their frustrations at former places of employment, and to share with one another how they want to make contributions to Kellogg. They are asked to identify challenges that they see for Kellogg, and to make commitments regarding how they can help the company meet those challenges.

Second, Kellogg uses the *Peacock* story in video version as part of its community-relations efforts. Kellogg shares the *Peacock* story with outside groups in an effort to help educate the surrounding community about the company's commitment to a diverse, high-performing employee population, serving the needs of diverse customers. Kellogg especially likes the emphasis on diversity as dealing with the whole person, not just race and gender.

And finally, Kellogg uses the *Peacock* book in their company tool kit on diversity, making the book available for employees via the company intranet. Employees can check out the book and read it as part of their ongoing employee development.

Maryland Fire and Rescue Training Institute

So, what do peacocks and penguins have to do with fire-fighters? Good question. We asked that question of the trainers and instructional designers at the Maryland Fire and Rescue Training Institute, because they have been buying hundreds of our books. Here's what the firefighters told us:

Because human beings are so diverse, their differences can cause conflict in tight communities like fire departments. But personal safety and survival depends upon overcoming these differences and working interdependently. Their teamwork is not like a track team; it is more like a football or baseball team. They have to rely on one another in high-stress situations. And they usually cannot pick the people with whom they want to work; they have to take the people they have and make them into a team.

The Maryland Fire and Rescue Training Institute uses the *Peacock* book to help teach fire officer candidates how to understand and work well with others who are different from themselves. The Institute's Fire Officer Management Certification Program is designed to help fire officer candidates identify their own work styles, and the work styles of others in their groups. The goal is for candidates to assess their strengths and weaknesses in order to build team effectiveness, especially in dangerous situations. Participants in the program read *A Peacock in the Land of Penguins,* then complete a "Birds of Different Feathers Work Style Assessment" (see "Training Materials" in Part IV on page 143), and engage in experiential exercises in order to build their skills at working in diverse teams.

The U.S. Department of Defense has accepted the National Fire Protection Association's standards, and has made arrangements with the University of Maryland to train uniformed military fire officers, as well as civilian federal fire officers. This well-designed training program is being adopted by other states as well. Fire departments in Oklahoma, Michigan, Colorado, and several other states have followed Maryland's lead in using a creative metaphor to bring home an important point about teamwork and differences, in the context of fire protection services.

Chevron Information Technology Corporation

Effectiveness in working with diversity (among coworkers, vendors, customers) has been identified by Chevron as one of the core career competencies for employees at all levels within the organization; but teaching everyone to be "diversity-fluent" was a major challenge, due to geography, language differences, and other factors. How do you begin to teach people about the importance of respecting and working well with others, when you have 26,000 employees scattered across 28 countries around the world?

Chevron Information Technology Company (CITC) faced these challenges by developing a diversity Web site, streaming the animated video version of *A Peacock in the Land of Penguins,* and using the "Birds of Different Feathers Work Style Assessment" (see "Training Materials" in Part IV on page 143) as an online interactive learning exercise. The Web site was pilot-tested with CITC's 1,500 employees, and as part of the launch, everyone was given a little four-inch-tall squeezable penguin stress toy. The program has been so popular that new hires at CITC often ask, "I understand I'll be getting a little penguin, too, right?"

The successful Web site is now enterprise-wide, in constant use by Chevron employees around the world. One middle-aged white male manager e-mailed his comments about his experience on the Web site: "I used to be cynical and bitter about diversity, because I thought it didn't include me. Now, after seeing the film and learning the story of the peacock, I see that diversity *does* include me. Count me much less cynical and bitter."

St. Peter's College

St. Peter's College in New Jersey has a special fondness for our *Peacock* story. The college is in the Division I Athletic Conference, and their mascot is a peacock!

St. Peter's vice president of Student Affairs used the story of Perry the Peacock in an off-site, overnight retreat she conducted for the Student Affairs staff. The staff members had just completed a lengthy process of strategic planning for the Division of Student Affairs, and were now ready to begin implementation of their five-year plan. Their most important challenge involved finding new ways of working together with other divisions at the college. Their goal was to foster teamwork among all the divisions, in order to better meet the needs of students.

Student Affairs staff members told us, "We have diversity all around us: new people in our division who have new ideas about how to do things; new relationships to forge with other divisions that have their own priorities and agendas; and certainly diversity among our students." They were inspired by the adventures of Perry the Peacock and his friends, and used the story as a metaphor for planning the future of the college and the Division of Student Affairs. Several task forces were formed, and they are presently hard at work, creating the Land of Opportunity for staff, faculty, and students at St. Peter's College.

Part IV

Additional Resources for Peacocks and for Penguins

After reading *A Peacock in the Land of Penguins,* people often ask, "What can I do to transform my organization into the Land of Opportunity? Do you have any tools, training materials, or other resources that can help me?"

The answer is, "Yes, we do." This final section of our book contains many resources for managers, supervisors, human resource professionals, and consultants to use in bringing about desired change in teams, departments, and entire organizations. Animated videos, assessment tools, a facilitator's guide, and additional books are among the many resources we have available. Browse through the following pages to find the appropriate items for your work situation.

Additional Resources
Are Available from

Peacock Productions
701 Danforth Drive
Los Angeles, California 90065

Phone (323) 227-6205
Fax (323) 227-0705

www.peacockproductions.com

Training Materials

"A Peacock in the Land of Penguins" video (11 minutes)

This best-selling animated video has been a consistent hit with organizations of all types and sizes. It has achieved the status of "classic" and is used in seminars, conferences, team meetings, and training sessions. The story deals not only with creativity, but also with change, innovation, teamwork, openness to new ideas, organizational flexibility, and diversity. The video comes complete with "Leader's Guide," including training designs on empowerment and diversity, seminar exercises and handouts, and a bibliography.

"Pigeon-Holed in the Land of Penguins" video (10 minutes)

This charming animated video is the perfect addition to any consultant's tool kit, or training department's video library. The video deals with the problem of pigeonholing in organizations, and explores teamwork, creativity, and the importance of seeing beyond stereotypes to maximize the opportunity for everyone to contribute to the organization's success. The video comes complete with "Leader's Guide," which includes training designs, exercises and handouts, and a bibliography.

"Birds of Different Feathers Work Style Assessment"

Are you a hawk, an owl, a peacock, or a dove? This work-style assessment helps you determine what kind of bird you are! Simple, quick, and easy to use, this self-assessment tool is enlightening and entertaining, as you see what kind of feathers you have, and learn how to work better with "birds" who are different from you. The instrument also includes a group assessment, so you can determine the prevalent work style of your department, team, or organization. It's perfect for individuals who seek self-understanding, as well as for training seminars on teamwork, creativity, communication, leadership, and diversity.

"The Penguin Index: Assessing Management Practices in Your Organization"

Do you work in the Land of Penguins, or the Land of Opportunity? This instrument is designed to assess your organization's culture and management practices — simple (25 questions), easy to administer, works well in training seminars or as an employee survey. It includes strategies for management, as well as positive tips that employees can use to make a difference in their organizations.

"Diversity Workshop Facilitator's Guide"

This comprehensive training manual includes guidelines for conducting effective seminars, as well as step-by-step instructions on conducting employee surveys regarding management practices in the organization. It also includes a section on career coaching, emphasizing diversity and organizational fit. The Guide comes complete with several training designs, seminar handouts, classroom exercises, overhead transparency masters, and a thorough bibliography of books, videos, audiotapes, journal articles, and additional resources.

"Diversity Dialogue," audio program (80 minutes)

This informative audio program features BJ Gallagher Hateley and Warren H. Schmidt discussing many different aspects of the complex issue of diversity. It is a lively, entertaining, and educational dialogue, designed to give the listener an overview, or "crash course," on diversity — both from a personal point of view and an organizational point of view. The audio program comes with a self-study and discussion guide.

"The Blame Game" video (10 minutes)

If you want to create a work environment where people innovate and try new things, you also need to be prepared for mistakes and problems. Taking risks is part of innovation, and taking responsibility is an essential part of calculated risk-taking. This creative animated video will help show you and your organization how to start finding solutions (rather than blame) when problems occur. The video comes with "Leader's Guide," including training designs on "Personal Accountability and Dealing with Change" and "Personal Accountability and Teamwork." Handouts, quizzes, and background material make this video and "Leader's Guide" a complete training package.

Merchandise

Penguin Stress Toys

Adorable, squeezable four-inch-tall penguins are the perfect outlets for your day-to-day stresses. Scrunch them down and they pop back up again. Throw them against the wall, and they bounce off harmlessly. Take out your frustrations on them — they can take it!

"Magic" Penguin and Peacock Coffee Mugs

These unusual coffee mugs show a row of penguins against a dark blue background. When you pour in hot liquid, the blue background magically turns transparent, revealing a glorious Perry the Peacock with the words "Show Your True Colors!" among his tail feathers. A practical, everyday reminder of the message of being valued for who you really are.

Feathered Pens

Big, brightly colored feather plumes with the message "Show Your True Colors!" bring home the message of being true to yourself. Assortment of colors; 18 to 20 inches long, depending on length of feather.

"E Pluribus Maximus" T-shirts

Colorful T-shirts silk-screened with one of the most popular images from the Peacock book, a gathering of many different birds under the banner of "E Pluribus Maximus (Greatness from Many)." The T-shirts are white, with a six-color silk-screen design. Available on an individual basis or in volume quantities for seminars and conferences, in sizes L and XL.

For Keynote Speeches, Training, and Consulting Services

Please Contact:

Peacock Productions

701 Danforth Drive

Los Angeles, California 90065

Phone (323) 227-6205

Fax (323) 227-0705

www.peacockproductions.com

PeacockHQ@aol.com

The Story Behind the Story

"How did you come up with the metaphor for your story?" people often ask. "The peacock in the Land of Penguins is so perfect — how did you think of it?"

The answer is very simple: I lived it. I was working at a large metropolitan newspaper in the late 1980s and early '90s; we held regular meetings of the executive and middle-management groups to review circulation figures, assess advertising revenues, and plan new goals. These meetings were always the same: The president with all his vice presidents and directors would sit in the front row in the elegant auditorium, and the publisher would begin the meeting by introducing each of them. One by one, they would pop up out of their chairs and turn to face the 200 middle managers in the rows behind them. They all wore dark suits, white shirts, and business ties; they were all about the same height, save one or two tall ones; and all but one were white males (the lone female penguin wore a dark suit and pearls). By all appearances, you would think they all went to the same barber and the same tailor!

One morning I was sitting in one of these meetings, watching these fellows like so many jack-in-the-boxes popping up, one right after another. "Huh!" I thought to myself, "they all look like penguins." Then I looked down at myself. I was wearing my favorite Carole Little dress, a bright and bold floral, mid-calf, a bit flouncy (but very slimming). "What's wrong with this picture?" I asked myself. "I'm like a peacock in the midst of all these penguins!" I shook my head, wondering how this could have happened. How did I end up here?

Thus the metaphor was born. Over time, I discovered others in the company who were in a similar predicament; the bird metaphor fit them, too. Helen the Hawk was a friend who was always criticized by her bosses for being too aggressive. Mike the Mockingbird was incredibly talented, and attracted by bright, sparkling new ideas. He frequently got himself into trouble by crossing functional boundaries in hopes of implementing his creative ideas. Edward the Eagle was an impressive guy from a rural state who was extremely smart but did not have the fine polish of the penguins. They let him know in subtle and not-so-subtle ways that he was not classy enough to make it to the top. Sara the Swan was sort of a dreamer, soft-spoken, with many good ideas, but viewed as flaky and unrealistic by the penguins. These were not fictional characters. They were all real people, struggling with the same problem I was — trying to be successful in a corporate culture that did not value creativity, innovation, and risk-taking.

This company was an extremely conservative place, with definite norms about "the way we do things here." None of us odd birds had a snowball's chance of being accepted by the penguins. Over time, we each came to the same conclusion, and one by one we left in search of our Land of Opportunity elsewhere.

All of my exotic bird friends are still in the newspaper business today — they simply found companies that valued their unique styles and creativity. I am the only one who did not stay in the newspaper business, but rather went into the writing business. It started with writing this book about my experience at the paper, and it continued with the sequel, *Pigeonholed in the Land of Penguins,* and the prequel, "Ruffled Feathers in the Land of Penguins" (in *Working Together,* edited by Angeles Arrien). Warren Schmidt has been a wonderful collaborator on all these "bird books." From our books came animated video adaptations, training materials, seminars, workshops, and fun merchandise like feathered pens, magic penguin mugs, and colorful T-shirts. The peacock and penguins have become a cottage industry unto themselves.

Probably the most gratifying aspect of this is the response we've gotten from readers, not just in the United States, but around the world. We get fan mail and email from people in many types of organizations, large and small, businesses and nonprofits, police and fire departments, schools, hospitals, universities, Fortune 500 companies, and many more. They all say basically the same thing:

"Thank you for telling my story. This is how I feel working in my organization. Your book reassured me that I am not alone. I have hope that I will find my own Land of Opportunity."

We also get international fan mail, with the greatest response coming from Latin America. Letters arrive from Mexico, El Salvador, Colombia, Brazil, Panama, and other Latin American countries on a regular basis.

- "God bless you for writing this book," some say.

- "Thank you," one woman wrote, "you have helped me get through these days in a very difficult organization. The penguins here crush my spirit."

- "Your book helps me understand people better and to become a better manager of all different 'birds' who work for me," another writes.

Warren and I agree, letters like these are the real reward for writing books. Royalties are nice, but touching people's lives is priceless.

BJ Gallagher Hateley
September 2001

About the Authors

BJ Gallagher Hateley

BJ Gallagher Hateley is much like the lead character in this fable — colorful and extravagant, noisy and messy — a bird who is difficult to ignore. She is a free spirit who loves her work — a child of the '60s who sees her mission in life as "comforting the afflicted, and afflicting the comfortable" (a line she once heard in a good sermon). She does both of them very well — especially the latter. She is a human-potential missionary who hangs out in corporations and other organizations, showing people how they can do well by doing good.

Her doctoral studies in social ethics at the University of Southern California (USC) equipped her to be a professional do-gooder, while her years in the business world taught her how to speak the language of the bottom line. She considers herself to be a pragmatic idealist. Her undergraduate training in the social sciences taught her to observe, listen, ask good questions, and analyze human behavior in all its complexity and paradoxes — great preparation for a life in business!

BJ was reluctant to leave the academic nest (she wanted to be a professor when she grew up), and spent seven years on the staff at USC — her last position there was director of Staff Training and Professional Development. While she was supposed to be writing her dissertation, she published a pop-psychology/pop-religion book called *Telling Your Story, Exploring Your Faith* (it paid better and was more fun).

She finally decided to try her wings in the "real world" of business, and landed at the *Los Angeles Times,* where she spent almost five years as the manager of Training and Development. It was at the newspaper that she developed a keen interest in studying other types of "birds," and she learned a lot while directing training programs and consulting projects for the company. She left the *Times* in 1991 to form her own consulting and training company, Peacock Productions.

Like any good peacock, BJ loves an audience, and is a popular workshop leader and public speaker. She really shows her true colors when she's talking about some of her favorite subjects: innovation and creativity, workforce diversity, leadership skills and success strategies for women, customer service, dealing with change, personal accountability, and her all-time favorite — how to manage your boss! She also consults with organizations on other human resource issues, such as team building, employee surveys, and strategic planning. She has managed to put on her penguin suit often enough to work with many respectable corporate and nonprofit clients, ranging from DaimlerChrysler, Kellogg, Chevron, and IBM to the American Press Institute, the City of Santa Monica, and the American Lung Association.

BJ has also written quite a few books. In addition to this one, she and Warren wrote two others: *Pigeonholed in the Land of Penguins* and *Is It Always Right to Be Right?* With Eric Harvey she wrote *Customer at the Crossroads,* and with Franz Metcalf she wrote *What Would Buddha Do at Work?* She even wrote one without a coauthor (it wasn't as much fun, though) called *Witty Words from Wise Women.*

This iridescent and irrepressible bird is a Southern California native, and is one of the rare people who really loves L.A. She is the proud mom to Michael, a young rock musician (what else would you expect in L.A.?). Her favorite song is "I Gotta Be Me."

BJ Gallagher Hateley can be contacted at:

Peacock Productions
701 Danforth Drive
Los Angeles, California 90065

Phone: (323) 227-6205
Fax: (323) 227-0705

www.peacockproductions.com

PeacockHQ@aol.com

Warren H. Schmidt

Warren Schmidt looks like a penguin and likes to think of himself as a peacock. He's really quite advanced in years ("chronologically gifted," he calls it) but has six grandchildren who force him to keep playing basketball, baseball, and tennis as if he were only middle-aged.

In his long career Warren has played many roles — from minister to psychologist, professor to city commissioner, researcher to screenwriter. He has taught others how to do life planning, but his own career has been shaped by a lot of unexpected opportunities — leading him from Detroit, Michigan (where he was born), to Missouri, to New York, to Massachusetts, to Ohio, to Washington, D.C. — and finally to settle down in the San Fernando Valley in California with his family of one wife (Reggie) and four kids, now increased to a clan of 16. While in California he has taught at two of that state's great educational institutions, the University of California, Los Angeles (UCLA), and USC. Even when he "settled down" at UCLA, however, he didn't stay with a single role, but moved from the Psychology department to the Graduate School of Management, where he ended up as dean of Executive Education. After 22 years, however, Warren finally became a mature, dependable professor of Public Administration at USC (but not quite a penguin, he insists!).

Warren likes to write — particularly with someone else. He first tasted the fun of collaboration when he and Bob Tannenbaum wrote an article on "How to Choose a Leadership Pattern" for the *Harvard Business Review* — a management classic that has sold more than one million reprints. He has written books on teamwork with Gordon Lippitt and Paul Buchanan, monographs on managerial values with Barry Posner, and most recently, two books on Total Quality Management with Jerry Finnigan of the Xerox Corporation: *The Race Without a Finish Line* and

TQManager. When BJ Hateley and Warren teamed up to write this *Peacock* tale, it began another delightful creative partnership that became even more interesting when Sam Weiss got into the act!

A major dimension was added to Warren's life in 1969 when he wrote a parable about divisiveness in America titled "Is It Always Right to Be Right?" Its appearance in the *Los Angeles Times* attracted the attention of four film producers (as well as Ted Kennedy and Spiro Agnew). Steven Bosustow (of *Mr. Magoo* fame) made an animated film of the parable; Orson Welles narrated it, and it won an Academy Award in 1971. As an "instant expert" on films, Warren was invited to become an adviser for CRM Films, and has never stopped writing and advising. (CRM Films produced an animated video of *A Peacock in the Land of Penguins* in 1995 and *Pigeonholed in the Land of Penguins* in 1999.)

As chairman of the World Heritage Foundation, Warren is currently helping to produce a series of TV documentary films on UNESCO-designated World Heritage Sites as part of the foundation's mission to "share and preserve the wonders of our world."

He also teaches an occasional course at USC and continues to speak, consult, and conduct seminars through his little company, Chrysalis, Inc., 9238 Petit Avenue, North Hills, California 91343.

Sam Weiss passed away in spring 2001, before this third edition was completed. But he made an important contribution to this new book before he died — he drew a fabulous new peacock for the front cover! We miss Sam and wish he were still here to enjoy the continued success of our *Peacock* story. Here are some things we would like you to know about him:

Sam was a distinguished dropout from both the Rhode Island School of Design and the Art Center College of Design. Their deans tried to persuade him to stay and finish school, but his calling was elsewhere — he had pictures to draw and films to make.

He brought a unique artistic style to the illustration of books and other print materials, adding a charm all his own. With the touch of a pen, characters came to life; with the stroke of a paintbrush, whole worlds began to unfold. In addition to being a versatile artist, he was also a musician, film director, scriptwriter, and all-around creative spirit.

Sam was probably best known as one of the preeminent directors in the animation industry. He wrote and/or directed numerous business-oriented training videos, including *The Winds of Change, To Try Again and Succeed, That's Not My Problem, I Told Them Exactly How to Do It, The Race Without a Finish Line,* and *The Blame Game.* His last production was *Pigeonholed in the Land of Penguins,* for CRM Films.

The films he directed have been honored all over the world, including an Academy Award nomination for The *Legend of John Henry,* sung by Roberta Flack, with music by Herbie

Hancock; and a Television Academy Emmy for *The Wrong Way Kid* (which included four adapted children's books). He won the Gold Award of the Art Directors Club of New York, Outstanding Film of the Year at the London Film Festival, First Prize at the Zagreb International Film Festival, the Jack London Award, and numerous other awards and honors.

Sam began his career as art director and designer on *Mr. Magoo* and *The Bullwinkle Show,* and within a few years was directing one of the hottest animated series of the late '60s, *Hot Wheels.* He moved on to Bosustow Entertainment, where he directed more than 50 films, including four CBS one-hour specials, which required adapting 30 children's books to animation. He also produced and directed 35 *G.I. Joe* episodes for Marvel and was a sequence director on the critically acclaimed *Little Nemo* animated feature.

During his career he directed the voice talents of Carol Burnett, Alan Arkin, James Earl Jones, Milton Berle, Rob Reiner, Mickey Rooney, Stan Freberg, Patrick Stewart, and other notable actors and singers.

Sam's wonderful wife, Marjorie, still resides in their home in Santa Monica, California.

Acknowledgments

This book reflects the creative thoughts of many minds and the encouragement of many hearts. This page mentions only a few of those to whom we owe so much.

First and foremost is Steven Piersanti, a kindred spirit who is a joy to work with. He saw the potential in our simple story and was willing to take a chance on this oddball book. Working with Steve has been a true partnership; his thoughtful suggestions (and tough questions!) helped us expand our thinking and develop our work over three editions. We are grateful to Steve for his continued support of *Peacock*; we are pleased that his initial gamble on our book is paying off.

Thanks also to the entire team at Berrett-Koehler — everyone has invested much time and energy in making our book successful, both in the United States and internationally. We are grateful to Pat Anderson, Kristen Frantz, Mike Crowley, Jeevan Sivasubramaniam, Robin Donovan, María Jesús Aguiló, Rick Wilson, Heather Vaughn, Ginger Winters, Bob Liss, and everyone else at BK. What a terrific team of wonderful people!

We also wish to thank the real-life "exotic birds," as well as the "penguins," whose experiences inspired our corporate fable. They will undoubtedly recognize themselves and the roles they played in the Land of Penguins. Extra thank-yous go to Phyllis Pfeiffer, Jim Shaffer, Larry Strutton, and Jeff Hall — who were especially helpful in the initial shaping of our story.

Special thanks, tinged with sadness, to Sam Weiss, who turned out to be much more than an illustrator — he became a cherished friend and creative collaborator on this project and several others. Sam passed away six months before this third edition was published, but we are happy that his drawings continue to bring our birds to life. We miss you, Sam.

And finally, a very personal thank-you to our families, who provided continuous support, encouragement, and helpful critiques as our fable took shape. Their love and attention nurtures our creative spirits.

158

Berrett-Koehler Publishers

BERRETT-KOEHLER is an independent publisher of books, periodicals, and other publications at the leading edge of new thinking and innovative practice on work, business, management, leadership, stewardship, career development, human resources, entrepreneurship, and global sustainability.

Since the company's founding in 1992, we have been committed to supporting the movement toward a more enlightened world of work by publishing books, periodicals, and other publications that help us to integrate our values with our work and work lives, and to create more humane and effective organizations.

We have chosen to focus on the areas of work, business, and organizations, because these are central elements in many people's lives today. Furthermore, the work world is going through tumultuous changes, from the decline of job security to the rise of new structures for organizing people and work. We believe that change is needed at all levels—individual, organizational, community, and global—and our publications address each of these levels.

We seek to create new lenses for understanding organizations, to legitimize topics that people care deeply about but that current business orthodoxy censors or considers secondary to bottom-line concerns, and to uncover new meaning, means, and ends for our work and work lives.

See next pages for other publications from Berrett-Koehler

301 Ways to Have Fun at Work

Dave Hemsath and Leslie Yerkes
Illustrated by Dan McQuillen

In this entertaining and comprehensive guide, Hemsath and Yerkes show readers how to have fun at work—everyday. Written for anyone who works in any type of organization, *301 Ways to Have Fun at Work* provides more than 300 ideas for creating a dynamic, fun-filled work environment.

Paperback, 300 pages • ISBN 1-57675-019-1
Item #50191-386 $14.95

301 More Ways to Have Fun at Work

Dave Hemsath

In this follow-up to the successful *301 Ways to Have Fun at Work,* Dave Hemsath applies the concept to new areas of business life to bring even more fun to the workplace. Like its predecessor, it combines thorough research with practical hands-on tools for using fun in the workplace to create a more productive and satisfying work environment. Over 300 real-life examples of how individuals and organizations have successfully instilled fun into the workplace make this book immensely practical and fun to read.

Paperback, 255 pages • ISBN 1-57675-118-X
Item #5118X-386 $15.95

Whistle While You Work
Heeding Your Life's Calling

Richard J. Leider and David A. Shapiro

We all have have a calling in life. It needs only to uncovered, not discovered. *Whistle While You Work* makes the uncovering process inspiring and fun. Featuring a unique "Calling Card" exercise—a powerful way to put the whistle in your work—it is a liberating and practical guide that will help you find work that is truly satisfying, deeply fulfilling, and consistent with your deepest values.

Paperback original, 200 pages • ISBN 1-57675-103-1
Item #51031-386 $15.95

Berrett-Koehler Publishers
PO Box 565, Williston, VT 05495-9900
Call toll-free! **800-929-2929** 7 am-12 midnight
Or fax your order to 802-864-7627
For fastest service order online: **www.bkconnection.com**

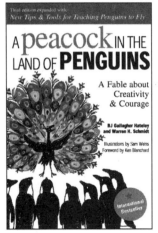